The Storm House

TIM LIARDET has worked in a wide variety of fields including cabinet-making, local government, economic development and higher education. In 2001 he taught for a year at the second-largest young offenders' prison in Europe. To date, he has produced seven collections of poetry. His third collection *Competing with the Piano Tuner* was a Poetry Book Society Special Commendation and long-listed for the Whitbread Poetry Prize in 1998 and his fourth, *To the God of Rain*, a Poetry Book Society Recommendation for Spring 2003. Liardet was awarded a Hawthornden Fellowship in 2002. He has reviewed poetry for such journals as *The Guardian*, *Poetry Review* and *PN Review* and has been the Poet-in-Residence at *The Guardian*. *The Blood Choir*, his fifth collection, won an Arts Council England Writer's Award as a collection-in-progress in 2003, was a Poetry Book Society Recommendation for Summer 2006 and shortlisted for the 2006 T.S. Eliot Prize. Tim Liardet has performed his work on BBC Radio Three and BBC Radio Four and read at many major festivals; he read at the Ars Interpres Festival, Stockholm, in 2007, and was visiting poet at the Internationales Literaturfestival Berlin, in 2008. *Priest Skear*, a collection that turns the drowning of the twenty-three Chinese cocklepickers in 2004 into a political allegory, appeared in 2010 and was the Poetry Book Society Pamphlet Choice for Winter 2010. He is Professor of Poetry at Bath Spa University.

Also by Tim Liardet

TIM LIARDET

The Storm House

CARCANET

First published in Great Britain in 2011 by

Carcanet Press Limited
Alliance House
Cross Street
Manchester M2 7AQ

A CIP catalogue record for this book is available from the British Library

ISBN 978 1 84777 067 7

The publisher acknowledges financial assistance from Arts Council England

Supported by
ARTS COUNCIL
ENGLAND

Typeset by XL Publishing Services, Tiverton
Printed and bound in England by SRP Ltd, Exeter

for my brother
David Liardet

Acknowledgements

Acknowledgements are due to the editors of the following journals and newspapers in which some of these poems first appeared, or will appear: *Agenda*, *Alhambra Poetry*, *Ambit*, *Ars Interpres* (Stockholm), *The Cincinnati Review* (US), *The Forward Book of Poetry 2008*, *Internationales Literaturfestival Berlin Programmjournal 2008*, *The Manhattan Review* (US), *The New Republic* (US), *New Welsh Review*, *New Writing 10*, *PN Review*, *Poetry International* (US), *Poetry London*, *Poetry Review*, *Poetry Wales*, *Salt Magazine*, *Slate Magazine* (US), *The Spectator*, *Stand Magazine*, *Sou'wester* (US), *The Times Literary Supplement*, *The Warwick Review*.

'Goose Flesh' was published both as poem and sound recording as part of the Slate Poetry Podcast in *Slate Magazine*, ed. Robert Pinsky and Maggie Dietz, November 2009. 'The Law of Primogeniture' was nominated for a Pushcart Prize (US), November 2008; four sections of 'The Storm House' were nominated for a Pushcart Prize, November 2009. 'Fantasia on the Snarl' was publicly broadcast for the first time on BBC Radio Three's *The Verb*, February 2008. The poem was commissioned by Bath Literature Festival, February–March 2008, and first appeared in the pamphlet resulting from the Festival. The particular notion of a disembodied snarl, at large in this poem, owes much to William Golding. Sections 3, 4, 13 and 19 of 'The Storm House' first appeared in *The Manhattan Review*, Volume 14, Number 1, Fall/Winter 2009-10. Sections 2, 6, 9, 18, 20 and 25 of the same poem first appeared in *Poetry Review*, Volume 99:4, Winter 2009. Sections 14, 23, 24, 26, 27, 29 and 32 of the same poem appeared in *Agenda*, Volume 45, Number 3, Winter 2010. Sections 5, 10, 12, 17, 22, 28 and 31 of the same poem first appeared in *Stand Magazine* 195, April 2011. 'Calling Ugolino', 'Sky Egg', 'The Beating', 'The Constables Call', 'The Gorse Fires', 'The Interlude' and 'The Water-halt' were published on the Poetry Society's Poetry International website, guest-edited by Kathryn Gray, August 2008. 'The Water-halt', 'The Constables Call', 'Fantasia on the Snarl', 'The Waterlily Garden' and 'Exit, Pursued by a Wolf' were translated into German for the Internationales Literaturfestival Berlin, September 2008.

Special thanks go to Molly Peacock for her very particular advocacy. I am grateful that this book has had the excellent good fortune to benefit hugely from the ears and eyes of Gerard Woodward, Richard Kerridge, Michael Schmidt, Peter Porter, and especially Fiona Sampson. The book is also for Miranda Liardet, without whose endurance and dynamic support it would never have been written.

Contents

My original scepticism concerning the possibility of speech reading had one good result: it led me to devise an apparatus that might help the deaf children...a machine to hear for them, a machine that should render visible to the eyes of the deaf the vibrations of the air that affect our ears as sound. It did not enable the deaf to see speech as others hear it, but it gave ears to the telegraph and you could hear a voice speaking, often at great distance.

Alexander Graham Bell, *Family Papers*, 1915

Like Slant Rain

Trouble is with inventing a language, brother,
when the only other person in the world who speaks it dies
you're left speaking to no one. This mouthful of words,

of fat verbs and vowels and cases and morphemes
that stammer from the lexicon under the tongue
is desperate to be used and anxious to be heard

and competes against itself for the room to speak –
It crowds out my mouth with the need to keep alive
every O in our intonation before it ends up

on the dump with the clicks of Hittite and Kulinic;
our words seem stranded and strangely marooned
now there's no one to read the other side of them.

No one to read them the wrong way round and still
have them make sense, say they are the wrong way round.
No one to say the old humanist's slanting hand

would not have wanted a mirror if he was the other side
but it's more necessary now, and I read in it:
lately, I confess, I've tried scrawling to myself in the glass

but, like any mirror-writing, it's slant rain. And like slant rain
it goes on falling and tearing, falling and tearing.
Like slant rain it quickens suddenly and slows down

and is heedless of its own expenditure.
Like slant rain it goes on falling and tearing, falling and tearing
and the glass does not know what it sees.

Calling Ugolino

Through what might be
the earpiece
or some grainier,
more primitive
instrument, brother,
or perhaps
the miracle
of the auditory
nerve, summoning
some signal,
a ruched pinhead
of decibels,
I imagined I might
be able
to hear your voice –
it would be faint
and strange,
belonging
as it does now
to another age,
the pauses
between it
prolonged by the whelm
of distance,
the static of water:
instead, the
soft voicemail
kicks in to say
you are
unavailable
to talk.
I had something
to say, I had
something
to say, I say
to the tape-hiss.

The Water-halt

The *sshsshssh*, the chambery smell of the dark
were borne from room to room by the Chapel official
in sniffs, her sideways glances, even in the look
with which she turned out of the candle's blue-ringed circle

with over-earnest tact: the crucifix above your toes
offered proportion to sacrifice – its striped dazzling image
waylaying the retina among the shadows
when I confronted your final, fuck-it-all visage:

you might have sat up, brother, but couldn't slip
the shackle of muscles which almost secured
a smile, thumbed and moulded to reshape
the malleable substance – your grim composure.

And for the more, there was only less;
and for your brow a freezing, terrible kiss.

Pity the police officers whose task it is to tell
the truth of the mysterious dying. They are pale
and gamine, they speak in unison like twins and might

be either men or women. One writes in invisible ink.
Mystery prospers, they say, when the eyes and the mouth
rest. The deceased's toenails had not been cut for months,

so long, they seem to grow longer now his body shrinks.
They're living evidence, say the officers, shoots of nail;
they arc in slow motion like the couch grass gripping

a plough that's blunted and abandoned. Is this a human foot
or some unusual specimen sprouting brambles,
sprouting sickles, until they hook right round

and scratch at their own footsole? This is what the truth
does, they say, it tickles itself to laughter at
our attempts to uncover it. His toenails force back

their cuticles like buds and might've hooked him bodily
back into the world just long enough to tell us
what happened in those final hours. The toenails are like the case,

they say, dark and horny, growing beyond our reach:
they grow and they grow, they flourish like clues
and curl back into accusation. Was he murdered at a height,

who could not stoop to tend them for himself?
So far below, wild and tapering, the toenails might
be protesting against the body's extreme inertness,

say the officers, they might be forming parabolas
of suggestion and still-growing questions or trying
to tell us the culprit's identity, like Nosferatu's
fingernails scratching a name on the air.

Grief-fugue

I play back at night the CD wiped by your death
because I want to gather in the snatches of *schtumm*

going round in my head all day, without making a sound:
I play it, I labour on the edge of remembering

the cellist miming the fugue – her bow sawing *schtumm*.
I play it again when the alternative's only

a silence plunging deeper through its calibrations.
Every time the disk spins, without sound, I feel

the fugue is enacted phrase by phrase, on mute
despite the laser's reading of everything there,

on mute so the noise of it is wholly turned down
though the signal's burnt deep, but registers nothing.

The disk plays and is *schtumm* – it plays and plays
or cannot quite stop itself from being played

and it when it spins from sound-pulse to sound-pulse
is exercised as it must be, trying perhaps to be rid

of the requirement ever to be played again –
I strain to read the label which spells out

in a childlike hand: *Schtumm for Cello*. And because
for all the life of me I cannot quite identify

the notes I feel in my fingertips, but cannot hear, I whisper:
play it again, play it again, play it again.

The Gorse Fires

I very gently drew out your brother's tongue
and placed it back again, said the coroner,
but began to feel it might have done it by itself.

Through the stethoscope, through the sternum,
he said, I could hear all the way to the sea bottom.
The eye with a torch shone into it – uninhabited.

What did he die of? That's the question I'm very glad
you've asked, he said. Ah, bodies – so many! Each one
more wiped, more stony-faced than the last,

pulled out in the drawer with a label tied to its toe.
Your brother might've died from drowning,
stroke, septicaemia, a shot from a range of half a mile

or, to put it another way, he said, the common cold.
The liver's bloated gland sifting its silts of salt
like moraines, like pond scum. Or spots on a tonsil.

The puckered arc of rips, he said, ousting the flesh
of his back like a crescent of bitemarks
that might have been a hoeing of six-inch nails

but, you must understand, they're merely braille.
Some bodies, he said, catch hold of the lies of the dead
and must be slid, unkissed, back into the drawer

while the outer world bursts with lively evidence.
The gorse fires blaze across the moor and kissing is
in season. But look at his mouth when a square of mirror's

held over it – nothing. It reminds me of a sign saying *privé*
at the gates of consciousness where no one had
trespassed for many years. Look to the living, he said. They should
be kissed and kiss often and live to be a hundred.

Versions of a Miserabilist

One thought, from over the river: the mosquitoes
lost the smell of blood in me half way across.

Old Eden verity – I am no more to blame for my death
than I was for the sleazy rendezvous of my birth.

God alters selfish men – now that they have no face,
he has them regard the face, he teaches them how

they should have lived in a universe whose every centre is
a little pot of self-regard, a little like yours.

*

This is the end of money, though we have black fingers;
this the seedy afterlife of things. Everything poised,

as if the next step were already on stand-by:
like a star in the cavity the pilot light keeps

the steady job of incremental burning.
The meter wheel spins round and round towards

the astronomical bill that will never be paid.
These are your concerns. The fridge, my symbol,

persists in its puddle and on-off fugue. Just when
you think it is finally dead, it rambles to life.

The Jigging Season

Craneflies hold up
a level sky
of stagnant water
on a hair:
lumbered
with ungainly
incarnation,
a convulsed,
electrocuted mess
of otherwise
lifeless limbs –
a fit of limbs
too slight
for the enormity
of life-fizz
inside it.
See how nothing
in their cells
has yet worked out
what glass is,
how they thrash
a paralysed
cortège of legs
against the glass
as if it were
the last obstacle
between them
and the next world.
As if glass
were a griddle
of six thousand
centigrade
making them jig;
and from here
they could already
smell the first frost.

The Law of Primogeniture

Whatever the planets were doing that second
they stopped, then resumed. The night
of the drop – the night of the touchdown

among the people he had chosen.
Jupiter and the full moon conjunct
opposing Mars. The void preparing

to match his likeness against the world's.
Vertigo for the very longest descent
of all, and motion sickness, jet-lag

and homesickness drawn down into one
mix towards the imminent focus of
a yell. The great scarlet hollyhock opened

and opened until it could open no more,
until the pressure ripped it at the rim
and my brother came into the world head first

on a deluge of his own making,
swinging limp bloody fists as if he was inconsolable –
Mother, son, swim forever in that blood.

*

Later by six hours, though, crouched thoughtfully
over the day's eighteenth stooping fag-ash
which is held up by a sort of freakish gravity,

my father is burning and poking the afterbirth
that crackles in the boiler like fat:
through the scorched glass he watches it burn yellow.

Though he shakes out the thought almost before
it skids beneath his thinning hair, he imagines
the afterbirth might be the sack

from which Rasputin emerged undrowned,
stones tied to his ankles and wrists.
So close, he squints into the flames' hysteria:

and he thinks his way back through
fags eleven, ten and nine, to where
he is running alongside the midwife's bicycle;

and he thinks his way further back
into the moment of conception, and imagines it
a single burning point of light;

he thinks his way back to the night he met her,
so overcooked with gesture – on the tilted floor –
so faux with shallow flirtation;

and he thinks his way much further back
through ten, through a dozen years
with giant stumbling, backward strides –

he stumbles back, muttering I must, I must
find a way back in time, in time –
out of the way you frowsty armchair –

you lamp, you flying – *fucking* – heirloom.
He stumbles backwards, like a man
doing backstroke with a chair in each hand,

a stool kicked out of the way by his right foot,
a pot kicked out of the way by his left.
He stumbles backwards, and just in time

(…against the timer's whirring) swings
one baggy trouser-leg over the other
and reassembles in the chair, from pieces, as the flash –

catching the lush valley of his parting
and good looks exploding in light –
goes off: *Me,* he whispers, *Me.*

On Pett Level Beach

Whether they look to east or west or straight ahead
with half-shut eyes, however stiffly caught,
they fall into place around her. She wears her white-rimmed shades,
                                               a two-piece,

but he's in trunks and overcoat and leans away and towards her,
smoking, with wild hair, under a laden post-war sky
which is streaked with light and goes on for miles.

One son in shorts with straps and bare shoulders, waiting
for the wind-mics to amplify her next command;
the younger son with spade, dragging seaweed around his ankles

into the foreground, about to walk out of the picture.
When Mother took the first son for her own, Father took the other
as if by doing so they enlarged the print of their terms:

as if, by doing so, he might chuck a single
futile weight against the tipping point.
All this in monochrome – vanishing from the plate;

all this to show you a family – so –
which huddles there, beside deckchairs which blow themselves
                                               pregnant;
as the sea smashes against the breakwater
and the breakwater smashes against the sea.

Goose Flesh

She climbed with the weeping boy
into the sleeves and legs of his clothes. He crouched

and acquiesced, and what he thought was his hand
reaching to pat the soft part of his abdomen

was in fact hers – her foot was in his shoe – so it was hard
to fathom if those scarlet toenails belonged to him

or her, and which body musk seeped out
from which armpit, which thought originated first

in his head or her encompassing head behind,
so little the lapse, the spaces, between them.

When he dressed himself, it was her hands that reached
around to each bone button, her fingers which clipped

the absurd butterfly to his collar. When she climbed out
and left a chilly shape where she had been

he felt his spine was corrugated and exposed,
every follicle of him, every single blond hair

always listening for her approach,
listening in all directions, from every hair.

When she climbed back, he could no longer feel
the coarse stitching in the seams of his shirt

nor any sensation in his feet at all
and no sensation in his hands or in his lips.

Where her warm belly brushed against his sacrum
he smelt of her cologne, and it was only

when he tried to shift his shoulders sideways
and fidget his body into a space

that her long arms folded across him from behind
and drew him back towards her, at which stage

they seemed to wrestle together in a canal sack,
one trying to keep the other where he was

by pulling the collar tighter against his neck,
one trying to escape from his shirt.

Jalousie

Into the arms of death, she says, into the arms
of another woman – who speaks the sort of patois

which alone could bind him to a pelt of bones,
whose pomp is laughable, her favours anyone's,

whose glad rags tend towards the sluttish
and whose half-moon grin, whose long enfolding fingers

combined one night to snatch away her eldest son.
Though her own legs by now can hardly carry her

to the otherwise bare outcrop of her eightieth year
she knows she has to match the slapper in her rags

and wants to buy new clothes, new fancy shoes
into which she might squeeze her water-swollen feet;

new rouge, new jewellery – flame orange silks;
new ear-rings – a crush of gleams however ersatz,

her mascara a sort of drenched French blue.
Voilà! She has begun an affair with the mirrors

by concentrating on that tiny square of face
that she dreams could still be made beautiful,

framed with hackles of hair, a sort of pout, a sort
of staging of mouth which forgets the fallow patch

of hair which even two mirrors, one held in air
and hand, one in front, cannot quite conspire to reflect –

as she applies a line of lipstick to her mouth,
leans in closer, plumps up the hackles. Ready.

The Ghost Train

Craneflies! she says. They fizz in and out of her face
and brush her forehead – the feelers. They're crackle-clumsy,

crashing, they trail their paralysed legs across the black hole
of her mouth, in sleep. They thump and sizzle inside

the mind's lampshade, she says – fortress mother –
they advance in a moon-halo of mints and halitosis.

Her hair so wild, so white, she goes among the gulpers
of a ward of daylight, frightening them with her tone.

Old! Old! she says. Everything old! Old as insects.
See how they fuss, she says, and won't be swatted away,

fizz, come too close. Or else, at other times, she says,
they're just a cotton bud fidgeting loudly in her ear;

some twitching thing fished itchily up her nostril;
some irritant in her tear duct, some frenetic thought

or jig of frenetic thoughts prancing over her;
the undercarriage of the nurse's flannel flying over –

this ceaseless intrusive business in her face.
Otherness! It bangs and struggles blindly against the glass

of a solitude that liked itself. It stumbles and blunders
and lurches all around her, it hums and shivers

as if it smells something it likes, it's in her bedclothes,
her smalls. Lord, bring us the extremity of the first

frost, she says. But look how easily legs thin as fuse wire
come away in her old, grief-stricken fingers.

The Revenant

This the door
opening from
the back of my neck
like a hatch
on a hinge:
(…you are such
a furtive, shifty
and insistent
ghost – you use
the hatch
like a cat-flap).
And this, brother,
your mewling
for food –
you expect
always to be
welcomed back,
while the flap
behind you
wipes out the last
of your tracks.
I must submit,
it seems,
to your taking
of death's steps
in reverse,
climbing the rungs
of my spine.
You climb so slyly,
so cagily,
as if to say:
where the ghost
comes to feed
through the hatch
there's a bowl.

Fantasia on the Snarl

The expression which I wish here to consider differs but little from that already described, when the lips are retracted and the grinning teeth exposed. The difference consists solely in the upper lip being retracted in such a manner that the canine tooth on one side of the face alone is shown; the face itself being generally a little upturned and half averted from the person causing offence.

Charles Darwin, *The Expression of the Emotions in Man and Animals*, 1904

Our remote Ur-uncles thought that cudgels were words.
The one hung up all morning by his braces on the kitchen door's
                                                                hook
and trying to kick at the universe like a tortoise in mid-air
was lied to by his father. This was not done for his own good.
Returned to the ground running, in furious impotence, he set off
the long curve of acts by placing the blame in his nephew, as if
he trapped him there beneath his boot and painted him in vengeance
from his head to his toes in scarlet paint. As if then the nephew,
deflecting the revenge, painted his brother a shade of pea green.
As if the pea green brother, in an impotent fury, held under in the
                                                                canal
the head of his cousin for what must have felt like a day
and watched hair swim all around him, painted, like his red face.

*

Poor boys, deep in the past, their oil paints were full of the lead,
the chromates, the cadmium, mercury and sulphides
that leaked like industrial froth into the family pond,
were carried when the level sunk, and entered the water supply.
Poor boys, waist-deep in the past, our bellicose forebears, kicking
from hook to kitchen hook, ducked and ducking others
and breaking out in rashes when the paint was scrubbed off,
                                                                learned how
they'd rather do it to others than have it done to themselves.
Though light bulged into their camera and filled the whole house,
though the wash of their lives barely survives the flash-gun and
                                                                makes them

seem the ghostliest suggestion of a people stood in a garden,
about to vanish from the plate forever, their reach is long;
the reach of their hands, the reach of their anguish and their fury is
long;
the reach of their brush-bristles, loaded with various clods of paint,
is long.

*

You were green, brother, you were red, the kitchen hook had grown
at the top of your spine like a bone spur, hoiking up your vertebrae:
at birth, though the midwife could neither see, nor wash it away,
you woke to find your nape and shoulder blades caked in paint, as if
the many stained fingers worked the pigments deeper
and the cruel male-to-male wounds inflicted along the curve
bled through your ankles and wrists. The power brought on the surge
in the brain's old gramophone and a man, yes, yes it was a man
began to sing frailly. He croaked about the laws of revenge –
but, for you, the targets he offered were too widely scattered,
led wider and wider, then crowded together the offenders
into the dark behind our father whose eyes you thought were stone.
So there were too many hands at once held you under
while your hair floundered, and I see you now, searching the sky
which slowly shifts from east to west its freight of altocumuli
and throws a stencil of it all across your face so palely
as a large bubble breaks at your mouth, two smaller at your nostrils,
and your underwater puzzlement seems to ask: *why me?*

The Beating

What you brought home to our mother no longer resembled
a human face – every follicle magnified
among the kick-marks, a Galapagos of kick-marks;
one half of your head swollen to twice the size

of the other, like something trying to get out,
something misshaping the cranium from the inside;
the upper heavyweight lip split open
like a plum into halves – the slit of the eye glimmering

under the monstrous lid. She laid out your body
and placed her hands into the water of the bowl.
Her name for you, she said, had stuck in her throat
like a wishbone that wouldn't go down and wouldn't come out,

and your legs so hairy, obdurate and bowed
would have to be shaved, she said, shaving smooth inroads
into the crop-roots of your body hair. That noise.
She removed the rags of your vest, like the hands

attending the holy body – she ploughed you through
with wild protective love, and you lay there,
saved. She raised your arms to wash them, and vowed
to go out into the world, that moment, to find the man

who'd pummelled and kicked you to this shape
and break him in two like the laws of forgiveness
and have him hobble and limp to the left
as her lumpen darling limped to the right:

and she was the snarl amplified at such a distance from
your mouth, and it was a snarl for a snarl.
It was furious steel capped boot for steel capped boot,
you might say. It was meat for meat.

'I thought it was a fucking earthquake,'

...said the milkman, whose mug of scalding tea slopped
into his lap as you stoved your Ford Prefect
up the float's rear end, from which a bridal train of milk
flowed to the kerb-edge of the full circle
which was the grassy island outside our mother's house
and would lead you back, by a few more degrees,
to the very point from which you started out
where she waved and waved you goodbye.
The pattern was scratched in the brain, you see, and you
watched the milkman sweep the confetti of glass
from the curve of the road which unwound to the north –
by which stage, glancing at your watch, you were
already back indoors implanting
the limp-stone in your sock, perfecting
the mirror-mime of a tremble.

The Interlude

What got you there – laid out in a cot, in a diaper –
was the scrum of punched nurses and policemen
who tried to restrain you as long as you flailed.
What were left, in the loose flesh of your arms, were

the bruises, as blue-purple as plums, like the footmarks
of the struggle that broke, flapped open and snatched
your mind. What I thought I'd heard was something
opening very abruptly and shaking itself out

in a rustle of ancient bodices and ballgowns
and corset bones which creaked. Whatever had flapped out of you
seemed to have taken with it the last of sense.
Whatever had flapped out of you, and gone its way,

had dumped you hugely on one side, one arm
laid limply over the other, oblivious to your visitors.
Whosoever lingered at the cot-bars – like the faces
in a Doré nightmare, uncertain of who stared at whom

and who stared back – you looked straight through
to middle distance, chewed on the cud of space.
Your son swayed away – this was too much for him.
By then all you could do was address your self

as if to say again you could not be reached,
and we felt like we were shouting and shouting
through layers of thick glass. We hoped to draw your mind –
by that I mean the wholly disembodied self

which might have hovered over you –
back towards the light…but had to leave, instead,
to the sound of your voice spinning in the dark
at the slightest touch, at the slightest touch.

Bucko in Love

The dog had the love, and gnawed it to the marrow,
absorbing it all. It drank love into the roots
of its unthinkable purple skin. There was a sense

of how love softened its ferocity and long tooth;
how it was turned cow-eyed and lugubrious;
how the love it absorbed became something else,

perhaps, a sort of pact, a covenant made
by the three who combed it, brushed it, fed it
and expected it to ingest their need.

Its whiskers wet with droplets of fog,
its wolfhound tongue slipped sideways
over the molars of its ancient grin. It secreted

the want of mother, brother and father
in its sweat-glands. They loved it so much, at times
it seemed the dog would swallow them whole.

It always answered, never spurned their attentions
or doubted it existed for them. It grew
three heads – one for each of them in turn,

and had no head for me. I knew it knew I knew.
I envied the dog for being doglike
and more worthy of love. I drew the saw's teeth

across its midriff, sprinkled it with hot water
so that it winced and cowered away.
Eating raw meat, acquiring a sense of smell,

trying to think of ways of hoovering in the dirt
and of developing unnatural tastes
at length I tried to become the dog

but it remained itself, looking back at me:
I dreamed its ribs creaked slowly apart
and opened like a gate on the garden.

Exit, Pursued by a Wolf

I can't quite recall what you did, but you'd done it
and ruined the party for everyone. Some had left
early, while injured Anne sat with her head in her hands
surrounded by a group of women with folded arms,
hunched together, exchanging oaths of sisterhood.
You were downing the umpteenth brandy when I found you
swaying and surly, and you swayed away in scorn
as I tried to offer yet another queasy homily
on the nature of decorum, as if I'd become
the holder of your overcoat, a runtish Feste,
an agony aunt advancing a plea for the common good
you wanted neither to hear nor ever act upon.
I followed you through a room of women
pointing into your face their fingers and accusations
which put the swagger in you, became a pride
as you walked through the door and I followed you out
into a warm, summer night. I was still talking
when you swivelled on me and threw me down,
threw all of your body's weight upon me as if you were
trying to smother something understood;
you held me down in the grass and punched me first
with the brunt of your fist, then the back of it;
you muttered close to my face like I wasn't your brother
nor anything to be loved. Then you stood up,
left me there like a punctured thing and walked off
rearranging your jacket, as if deserting a car-crash.
Later, back at home, as you often did,
you went up through the skylight of the bathroom to stretch out
on the roof-tiles under the stars
where I imagined you whispered an all-but-audible mantra
over and over to yourself: I know how to behave,
I know how to behave, I know how to behave.

The Waterlily Garden

Turning to weeping what was meant for joy...

Dante, *Canto XI*

I'll tell you about my shitty life, you said,
and then proceeded to list the grievances
you'd nurtured with care from seeds. You neither lifted
your head nor paused as a great roof of glass

displayed the old conservatory – its perfectly balanced
majestic presence shedding indoor rain and light
over the gongs of lily pads which were immense,
steaming, ablaze like mirrors. The racket of birdlife

turned itself up, and the drama of it all flourished there
in the gently shaken arcs of shadow-work
the roof's filigree cast over them and seemed to draw
a graph. Your mouth was striped and dazzling as you talked

and saw and heard nothing but your hands and voice,
your hands and your voice, beneath all that space.

Self-portrait as Flypaper

When they came home with empty pockets
yours were stuffed with rubbish – bits of carton crushed
into a gesture, say; yellow scraps of newsprint

coming into flower, old cigarette butts
held in their last agony – chewing gum
peeled off your shoe like a spun filament

until it snapped – all were stuffed in your pockets
as if you'd taken pity on them.
Each piece found on the pavement seemed

to call to you, as if it had further to go.
Your furious mother ended the reprieve
and scrubbed out your pockets, as if that might

wipe it from memory. They called you *flypaper*:
but you preferred to see yourself as the one who found
a cranefly in old fuse wire, a silkmoth

in a squashed butter bean – anything in a shed sole.
The family consensus set, like concrete,
against you. But you saw yourself as a special place

for garbage, full of holes that were defined
by a net within which the spaces filled up
quickly with blown litter, until you felt

you were becoming visible…or else these worthless scraps
were fragments of a language that offered you
the prospect of change, the whispered promise

of reinvention – open cigarette pack for jaw,
say, a mark-up price for one eye and bottle-cap
for the other, crushed tampon for a nose;

a torn off half of strap-line for mouth.

Self-portrait with Patio Flames

My mother and brother giggle on the patio
which is so intensely lit they're scarcely visible:
the light erodes them, it eats them away
but can't squeeze between them as they giggle

and whisper in the way that people do
when they meet no resistance in each other.
The lido and the Med burn up below –
his hair's freshly cut, and he wears the blazer

of my mother's choosing, sky blue. She wears
a floppy hat through the weft of which light
is cast in freckles over her neck, her hair.
When sea and beach are loud, the two of them cannot

hear the question I repeat three times, or so it seems.
They giggle and whisper though the day is in flames.

Sky Egg

Body and world were never the place
for you to live in. There was climbing, though,

climbing not out of the body but out of world –
in the fork of the tree, so high up it seemed

you'd already got to the sky and I was gravity
in your shoes. I kept you upright by somehow

contriving to be the counterweight far below
as long as you swayed up there. And as your arm went up

mine sort of pistoned down. As your arm reached down
mine was slowly raised, and you started back

towards earth with caution, a kind of guardianship
exercised by every nerve tensed for falling

in your body, and placed the sky egg carefully
between your teeth; you placed it there so tenderly

and eased yourself down backwards as if you were
responsible for bringing down to safety

the rarest and most susceptible outer shell
of life's longing for itself – so pristine and so sky-blue,

perfect, but for the faintest freckles of blood:
don't fall, I shouted up to you, *don't fall, don't fall...*

Now you fall through time, if not through time and space;
and the darkened freckles survive, are everywhere.

They are on your hands, on mine. They are on your shoes.
They were on our mother's wedding dress before you were born.

Deleted Scene (The Frog)

The terror lived in the shed, we knew. It was the buckled mirror
propped in the depths, in which the frog grew smaller and smaller;

poor frog, it dried up so slowly in our tin's evaporating wet –
too unthinkable to touch, too much to prod or handle, let

alone to sluice it with water. It was like a little old man –
a little old man with an old man's withered fingers and hands

that disturbed us to our hair-roots, while the spider on stilts of hair
stumbled over the nape of our necks and made us both shiver.

And I left you crouched at the door, brother, when the shed's
                                                             roof-felt
so pressure-cooked the terror, and grew so hot, it'd all but melt;

I left you crouched there once I had, considering how to, stepped
through the speckled sheen of frog and mirror in one step.

The step was long, and now you're dead, I find myself wanting to ask
for some primitive forgiveness – against the slit of sky, cirrus-flashed,

you were abandoned to a space less than half a metre square
and circled yourself repeatedly, or strained into the dark from where

it was always high August and the door-slit bulged a brilliant fog
out of which you stooped and grew smaller, face to face with the frog

that looked straight through you to where more than sun bulged in;
that was just the shape of its frog-mouth, I swear it, and nothing
                                                         like a grin.

The Brothers Grimm

There was milk though the dead had lost their thirst
and crates of it rattled in the early air
when we entered the chapel to find him
rouged in his long gown and coffin where

the big sprays were light and the hands of those
who wished to keep him with them got a grip,
and one of us took, one offered energy,
one kissed the brow which burned and froze his lip

and turned away, full of protein and iron,
out of the place in which the other stayed;
one of us took energy, took calcium,
one lay down smiling by his father's side.

Ur-blue

The last time I saw my father he had
the eyes of an angel. I do not say this sentimentally,
or in false hope, or even to imply I knew

before then what the eyes of an angel would
or would not be. But at least because his body seemed
as if it had recently come through the flames,

had walked through flames which changed the look of him
when his skin grew tighter as if it were burned;
because he brought up the wasted scarp of his knee

towards his chin in a jackknifing movement
and tried yet again to pull off his pyjamas
as if this might seem a normal thing to do –

his eyes were either the eyes of an angel
or did not quite belong to his body any more
as if he had somehow become another species

*

and was already no longer my father.
                    Do you think you know blue?
The colour for which the very shyest of all
of Stone Age tribes still has no word. His eyes were the source

of blue, where light discovered it, where blue sprang;
they were lapis lazuli – lit from behind;
they were gentian and cyanosis, sapphire and lavandula

bidding for the crush of molecules;
they were Prussian blue and cerulean, cobalt and smalt,
they were indigo and woad – they were all of these

and none of them, they were blue, more then blue;
and his pupils edged across like the soul's eclipse
and the blue around them bred in the way

that took it out of colour into something else.
His radioactive body from which the pounds had
fallen away like so much surplus clothing took the blue

and made it otherworldly at its own expense.
He looked at me then
                              as if I was
a newly cleaned window on the route he was taking.

A Portrait of my Grandfather in Drag

When all those who do not wish to play with him are left at home
he steps into the storm, the free-for-all, of chromosomes;

the future's a swarm of heat in the road – he so rouge-obsessed
we lumbering oafish boys might fear we'll never get to exist;

we fear he'll never get to fill the shoulders of his coat, or fit
the belt that here would wrap around him twice like a straitjacket;

he's an identity, he seems to imply, under construction
but for the time being is bits of self flung in all directions:

in Richmond, though, in what might be Nineteen-Twenty-Three,
or Four, it's lip-gloss, fan and feathers and bits that fly away

as the lippy girl, who so disturbs me, steps out of him to reveal
the forces perched precariously on that abyss-edge of stool –

I'm disturbed but curious and, through the magnifier, trace
the last centimetre of a hair that separates the uncle from the niece

and the niece from the angels. The flash explodes in the dark
and between him and it a daylight of reciprocated shock.

Look in any encyclopaedia. *Gender*'s a river in Noord-Brabant,
a gong struck in Javanese gamelan music and the agreement

of noun and pronoun, but tonight, says grandpa in his billowy silk,
the rest is so much glazed and so much slippery talk.

The Peacemaking

Your son, father, your elder son leant over
your eyebrows which rose slowly to meet:
from the open bedroom door I could overhear
him whisper: 'I'm *sorry, I'm sorry*...' You splayed your feet

then lifted a deathbed finger in a gesture
of not having heard a word, puffed your cheeks. The slit
in the blown blind shed light across your chest
as if cutting you in half – a perfect cut

made between gusts from the outer world.
These were the words he spoke to you, the very last,
and now he's dead, and the monkey tree which cast
the family tree underwater is felled:

the stump's all sprouting foliage, as if iron had blood;
as if blood were the peace that was never made.

The Vintage

Enough time, father, there was enough time
in the hour after you died for the family home
to flap itself all but free of its ropes,
to be flapped to its last remaining rope –
enough time, at last, for the two of us to purloin
your Bas-Armagnac brandy which had stewed
in its bottle for more than a hundred years,
getting darker, stronger, getting wickeder.
It was like a vault-door, the deep stopper,
eased open against its will. The spirit threw off
promise like the halo of Christ, we trembled it
to our lips, our tear-ducts were swollen, we thought
it might be the firewater of God. Once drunk,
the liquor's tongues began to wag through us,
all night we fought with our tongues like knives
for your all-but-weightless body, which had shrunk back
to its bones and made all your joints horselike;
all night we fought for your body, tossed it about
on the mob of our words until its shroud unravelled
as every word tried to rip at it for the last time
and filch some holy relic for itself.
Older than us, the grapes fermented
while you still circled the void,
and that night we invented new expletives, father,
we ripped at your sides and at each other
until we came out the other side of enmity
into a drunken scrummage of hugs,
we drained the bottle to a gaspy space, a gape,
a cave awaiting the sea. We drained it
to the bottom of our words and to the bottom of ourselves
and to the bottom of the world
as the night-coming officials stooped
and drew the body-bag's zip slowly over your face.

Deleted Scene (The Jug)

You'll never understand why your stepfather pressed you
to fill the jug with water to its fat lip,

those pale Chinese figures painted around its hips
ending the story only so it could begin again.

You listened through chin-length hair, the stepson
staring at the jug with a look which shifted quickly

between embarrassed, helpless and terrified –
You'll never understand why he asked you then

to smash the jug without spilling any water, break it,
he said, any way you want, but do not spill a drop.

You hugged its weight against you, felt water
slop down your shirt and onto your bare feet, let go –

when it smashed on the tiles into exploding bits
and flew everywhere as if somehow in slo-mo,

just for the briefest second the water held
a miraculous jug-shape and stood there on its own –

it trembled, trembled, as you willed it to –
before its hips broadened, brought it slapping to the tiles

and the splinters of china sprouted from your palms.
My hands, you said. My jug, he said, *my jug*.

The Dark Age

By the time the second plane blew up
all he knew was he was one of a new race
entering a new age, in need of water:
the cloud of ash bulged between skyscrapers

that seemed to lean closer and he knew
his brother was there at the source of it –
so he stopped, he did the strangest thing,
he took off his railway-worker's coat

to improvise a street-bed, he thought of
unlacing his boots but recalled how a toe
poked through his sock-hole, then turned the coat
inside-out with the satin to the light

and rolled it up slowly, put his head
to the pillow he had made – his brother,
he knew, was at the source of the cloud
so he lay himself down exactly where he was

there in the street, tucked up his knees,
smiled, or wore a face that nothing could name,
then slept as the snowfall of ash, petal
for petal, covered him and everyone else.

'...Lay Thee Down'

It came back to me quite suddenly – carrying with it the curl
and doubling-back of undertow, things said
in ignorance and later forgotten –
the day the curtains, brother, closed you away

and we stood chewing grief like rinsed lettuce.
Every night for as long as you and I shared
that back room – I said it to you;
loving the sound of the words which played out

excesses I could never quite put to sleep,
I said it, over and over again:
for the last time now goodnight, Davy;
for the last time now goodnight, Davy.

The Storm House

The only piece of action in the dream was the opening of the window, of its own accord; for the wolves sat quite still and without making any movement in the branches of the tree, to the right and left of the trunk, and looked at him. There were six or seven of them. It seemed as though they had riveted their whole attention on him.

Sigmund Freud, *From the History of an Infantile Neurosis*, 1918

1

There'll be beating on greenhouse panes, as if
such weight of water might get the dead to sprout and grow
but not yet, not yet, every stem stock still:
the trough's surface is unblemished and the bronze cupid
streaked with verdigris, toupee'd in stormflies.
I'm holed up for three days in this sequestered folly
which is stuffed full of guests, of luggage and staff.
The old hotel is full of people, the pool
of leaves. I am *away*. From east to west the thunder
grumbles from speaker to speaker, talks up
the showdown of storm and rain, storm and world.
When cloud crawls through the Mendips the lights come on
upstairs, in the tenth of a hundred rooms, still dim;
and you are not to be found in any one of them.

2

Sequestered brother, a year dead, now the world
must get by without you. If once you had willed
world and self into being, and looked for their limit, now
the world vaporises with the self. Let's say
you're further from home than me tonight. Out here,
estranged from my own life, I've the space to confer
with your rather untalkative absence. It might be
a sort of praying, or a speaking of terms which will
remove me further and further from the lobby:
the noise is far below, now that I've slipped away
and have to lift the dicky bar of the fire door
to retreat to my room, until a time rain through the glass
streams, like a ghost, over the hotel letterhead
which was never once intended to address the dead.

3

Untalkative brother, a year dead, everywhere world
is in the ascendant. Out here the air is heavy with rain,
the crowded lobby like a railway station.
Out here, estranged from world, I feel the urgency
to explain exactly what it was that happened to you
and to dig for the whole story, manhandle you back
into the frame and weigh you, measure you, thump
electric shocks into your body, smudge off
the mortician's make-up from your face and wipe away
all blame and false forgiveness. I want to rewind the flames
that flowered along your limbs, at finger and toe:
I want to walk you out of the furnace, put you together
as if by doing so I might be able to map
a way back for you, forward for me. Then let you sleep.

4

I want to suck back the hissing along its jets
like the flame-spirits forced to withdraw the flames
and find you whole, sit you up, winch you
in your collapsed kilos by your armpits and swing
from left to right the mickle hams of your fists:
I want to wrestle you back into the world and lift your chin,
so very gently, off your chest, detach the dark
lying close against the balls of your eyes.
I want to put you in shoes, stand you up, persuade
the tiniest buttons through your buttonholes
and, after the journey, have you speak a few gruff words.
But look at the tongue – that giant glib muscle slumped
into speechlessness, less instrument than bung
and unable to tell us one damned thing.

5

Talking to the dead's not easy. I'm robbed in daylight
of the gift of speech – any mouthful of words
as if cluttered out with stones impervious
to the seep of listening. Any word like a stone,
so smooth, so hard, nothing can soak into it.
Wittgenstein was right. A private language
is like the stone. I can talk of the birthmark exposed
by your hairline, those fingernails deformed
by years of chewing, but the stone absorbs nothing.
Whatever words I use are like rain that is yet to fall
responding to the shock waves of the thunder;
at the window, a dry spot in a future which rains:
along the ridge of the wall, moving fast,
the spun green and yellow dome of an umbrella is hurrying past.

6

The two policemen, seven foot tall, came to tell
our mother you were dead – their overcoats dripped
all along the Acorns' newly polished corridor
before their words, spoken softly, released the flash-flood
which set her arms flailing and ornaments flying
as she moved to knock the lanky messengers
flat on the slab where you lay, feet splayed.
A straitjacket was considered, but how could a bodice
that anchored her hands, a grope of straps, constrain
out-of-body grief? The constables read their shoes,
and the truth of your death was stubbed beneath them.
Fishy, said our beautiful Asian doctor, to the pharmacist
who said the same to the salesgirl, who seemed to say
such fishiness could already smell the sea.

7

It's fishy, said the chemist nodding to the nurse,
who nodded back. I saw him stride out with his dog
a day ago, said the meter man to the chemist, who nodded.
This was how the fame of your dying crept
like the scoop that never was, nod to nod, each version
further and further from the truth, as if you had
already died a hundred times. No suspicions,
said the police and coroner, when they tried to fit
the squeezebox of bodies folding itself up
into the slab's one body – but look, look,
said our mother, use both of your eyes to look:
cast them along the length of him and see how his murderers
are stooped around his feet in overcoats but still,
because the room is rather dark, almost invisible.

8

You lived among dangerous people. They were the men
who picked the bits from your overcoat
because they knew that shortly they'd be wearing it.
The overdose of coke they racked up, they knew,
would race mercury up the tube and leave you
dissolving from the fingertips, from the knees down,
all traces be gone from your body in twenty-four hours
and those who gave it you, this minute, know who they are;
wherever they are, this minute, *they know who they are.*
By the time it struck your central nervous system,
they knew, you'd be a universe of goodwill
and already at the limits of body and world –
not quite in the state to consider that
having gone beyond the warning boards, you'd have to get back.

9

Unprovoked, said our mother, the attack on you
a month before you died – the death before the death:
the stave with six inch nails driven through it
clutching the flesh of your back like the scourge's hooks
as you hugged your knees for protection;
as if those spikes tilling the soil of your back
were not considered a clue, as if wounds
more terrible, more disfiguring, might have been a clue.
Though such wounds appalled your doctor they drew
the mandatory nod, the shrug, of the police:
this was the way you were taught the imperatives
of justice in this world, how each nail which could
have punctured wrist and ankle had not spared
an inch of flesh against your broken word.

10

But then, the last time I saw you, I tried to punish you
by saying that I'd never expected to see
a brother of mine yelling among the cropped heads,
the yells of those with *Rest in Peace* tattooed
at the killing spot of the forehead. I told you how my snarl
might one day outsnarl yours, how I expected more
than the grim epithets for which your mouth
mimed the words almost perfectly. Since that
last sight of you, your face has haunted me like a lantern
hoisted half in shame, half reprimanded snarl –
At least it gives him an interest, said our mother,
as if you'd started collecting stamps, and spent all day
trying to decipher through a magnifying glass
the postmark obliterating the old queen's face.

11

All the old rhetoric found through your lost self
a gateway – the men slurping rutabaga soup
in striped pyjamas, those mountains of shoes
and spectacles, those sacks of human hair, you said,
mere props shifted into place for the hoax.
That's why you threw, not stones, but yells
at the crowded steps of the synagogue
and felt them clatter back down towards you.
When you told the judge how any Jewish piano could
be pitched into the street below and smashed
in the thousand gonging fragments of a dying fall
without so much the breaking of some sweat
you dreamt the moment of break-up, as the polished wood
shattered into spears and arrow-heads.

12

In the silence, when the whingeing subsided,
had our father uttered a few sly words, or flashed
a sickle of glances without words where he stood
stooping over your crib? Had he dreamt of digging
with his bare hands a hole that was deeper and wider
than imaginable, beneath the rug's buttercup yellow?
Had he vowed, for you, this would be no paradise
and placed stones and charms around your crib,
Inca teeth and arrowheads which were the ghosts
of dormitory chilblains, the ghosts of sobs, the ghosts
of the face like an art deco lamp casting a halo
for which he was sent away? Had the long pins
of his thoughts sharpened themselves most at night,
never to be spoken aloud in daylight?

13

At ten, as at fifty, you wore our father's necklace
of charms, under the skin. So many old revenges
were swung from your belt like scalped frogs, some still alive,
hooked through as if you were keeping them fresh.
And your impotent fury was turned, in turn, on those
you most resembled, the boy kicked in the doorway
into a deeper heap – the boy pitched through the glass.
The arms of remoter men flailed like a tree of fists
in your coat-sleeves, along with our father's unstruck blows;
they lunged under your arms and over your shoulders,
punched with you, and for you, though some blows
were merely struck against your body, and left
your ribs bruised and your ripped collar to wag
as if you were both puncher and punch-bag.

14

There were many journeys, there were half-journeys,
but that of the heart a pilgrimage in reverse,
a return to the source from which to set out again.
World conspired, as it always did, lamp-posts buckled
your bonnet and engine, trees moved into your headlamps;
you wooed danger only so you could return
to the chair shaped to your comfort, opposite our mother.
At twenty, as at fifty, you knew the ritual so well
there might have been marks for your elbow
and one for the placing of your foot, a pot
for your keys by the door – as if all the words
you could not speak out loud were written
in a letter slid beneath the only brick
in the whole house that was loose, rueing your luck.

15

The firmament stayed low, you felt, as if sky
were actually crawling all over your body:
the heat persisted – burning needles in your forehead;
you ripped off your clothes, stomped from room to room
and out onto the balcony, speaking garbage;
you were the naked man who terrorised a neighbourhood,
recharging Lear's *non sequiturs*, like lights,
and like Lear unable to say if your hands were your own.
The temperature rose, the pressure formed slowly
the idea of the weapon it placed in your hand:
as if you were (how to put this?) the pulses
of thunder all around you, and still the clock ticked,
the wallpaper moved, the cistern was full
and in the garden below the alders waited, stock still.

16

When the pressure broke, almost like relief, the blow
you landed on the fragile pot of her skull
was of such force it broke the stick in two. Her vertebrae
contracted her just a little more, her ankles
hardly able to support what mass she still possessed
fell from under her, her brooch unpinned and flew off
like a panicked bird, she flailed as if blindly
then dropped. When she dropped, you might have dreamt
she carried the identical likeness of you
in that dying fall, since first you linked hands where
you sprawled on her sternum, and grew to four to twenty to fifty
without once letting go, as if it were no more
than fingers which welded the clasp
and sent roots thirsting deeper, into the dark.

17

The words you let out, grumbling in the heavens,
will never be recorded. They slurred and went round
like little gasps of energy popping and babbling.
You see, I want to slow it down – the stick transformed
into a strobile of twenty walking sticks flowering
in one downward thrust, every billionth of a second
shown in slo-mo so I can see exactly
how it distilled the rhythm and logic of your life
into a single act, there at the far end of the sunlight
that stretched its way across the rug
and pulled itself out of shape. The reverberations,
the shock, the fear, the weapon that broke in half
as she fell to the rug which was so intensely lit,
I know I must tell it all, finally to be rid of it.

18

The stick came down from every angle,
there were twenty, no, thirty sticks, each seen from another angle,
each coming down empowered by the reason
for its own force, more vehemence here for this
less vehemence here for that, some regret here,
some grief, some asking-for-forgiveness,
but in that moment, I do believe, you most imagined her
sat in a wicker chair on some Bolivian balcony
watching insects over water, comfortable she was too far
from her sins to be blamed. And the damage done
by the blow, you were convinced, was a kind
of suitable punishment, a sort of justice.
It was justice that was energy, justice that was fuel;
it was justice that put the whip in the ferule.

19

The blow was delivered to the crown of her head,
made easier by her smallness. Skin and bone resisted
just for a second, as if it might hold before the blow
creased it into a furrow, and the skin at first
stretched to accommodate, then split apart –
her scanty, light-coloured, greying hair
smoothed thickly all over with oil as it always was
had been plaited into a rat's tail and gathered together
under the remains of a horn comb. As the blow
was delivered she fell, shed herself like a shawl.
Above her, you were spasms of light circling
the room below that rose around the slick of her blood.
This was the point at which you discovered a voice.
Moral arithmetic. One more requires one less.

20

Like something that cannot help but move
however injured, appalled, however hurt,
she climbed back to her feet. Raskolnikov's nightmare –
the old woman rising from the puddle of her blood.
And this the strange thing – the blow which had felled her
in the very manner it had been delivered came back,
came back, came back and struck you across the head
and split the skin of your cranium, blue bruises bloomed
all across your torso, and the pressure which
the blow had released was pushed back
into the chamber which created it, but worse now,
cramping your muscles. The blow came back, and almost
wrenched out from its socket the very arm
which had delivered it, sent back to where it started from.

21

I remember nothing, you said, I remember nothing,
I remember nothing. Said often enough, you thought,
you showered away the blood, you heaped up your clothes
along with your wallet and passport and flung
a match flaring sulphur – chewing in the light
of the flames, you said, you remembered nothing.
At night, wide awake, you pulled down the blind
but the sun still squeezed in through the weave
and bulged through the gaps. You taped them up
as if seeing and being seen were the same.
What seemed like the midnight sun buckled you
to only a squint. With it, the blow came back
as if trying to tell you the physics of revenge
was somehow spring-loaded, and creaked on a hinge.

22

The most important conversation we never had
dug the deep hole it might have occupied when
I received the news, and spoke into the mouthpiece:
you've done it now, I said, you've done it now.
Up the wall, you replied, she drives me
up the fucking wall...oh dear, it is so very hard
for you, I interrupted... At which stage you hung up, hung up
and would never speak to me again, and I was left listening
to the dialling tone which had an ironic sort
of sing-song note at large in it, and the low growl
seemed to deepen and now continues deepening,
goes on deepening one year after your death
as if it is smooth pebbles knock-knocking together
in the cold, the wolfish belly of the river.

23

Such lights as burn in the hotel, our mother's convinced,
attract you still. In death as in life, she says,
the old reverberations reach her. The flash-lamps bob
at the window, and your face is behind them;
your eye is at the peep-hole and magnified
twice its size, so blue – your fingers at the letter box.
In an apartment shuttered by dark glass,
she says, she follows the sounds through the wall
while each of those porcelain clowns you bought for her
holds up an instrument and farded look
as if playing a tune no one else but you can hear.
Faced with this disturbance which shakes
more than her pot of pins, you understand, I put on in my head
Tchaikovsky's *Danse Russe*, and turn it up loud.

24

Imagine the act of love, or will, which swings back
in a single lunging motion the heartbreaking distance
to the inch between nose and nose – yours and hers.
In this cycle, it seems, she has mistaken
darkness for daylight, and daylight for dark.
If one reveals to her the dew on spider silks
spot-lit by a low trajectory, the other draws up to her chin
a duck-quilt of unseeing. And they might
change places, they might pose as one another.
If I am the one who feels you watching me
and imagines you passing – like a spider on the stairs –
our mother's been reported missing from herself
and cannot quite trace back all that's been mislaid;
or what it is that has, has not been said.

25

The nights pour over and are not themselves
and where has she been, for all those hours? Wandering
in her nightdress, to the bottom of the garden
where just for a moment she might have seen you
where just for a moment she saw you
where she saw you, she says, like the Batalha Christ
– all torso, blown away at the knees –
visible only from the waist up, looking straight ahead;
where she saw you, she says, forming and unforming
in the vapours of low blood sugar, standing stock still
and relenting from under the firs into a sort
of smile, a sense of the yet-to-be-assembled
weighting the darkness behind the ash-cans
and weighing, weighing in your punctured hands.

26

The spooks, the offices of the dead, the stink
of the Chapel's lilies drifting from room to room
like a mild gas, the hole you have left which sets
the few who survive you hurrying to form
alliances that are new – all of these a single smell,
an atmosphere, the sort of chill which creeps
but cannot weight the hems of the few frenetic seconds
of Pyotr Illyich's thirty violins in full flight
free-riding me to joy, the spring and leap
of energy suddener than body and world:
now that I must see for two, I must attempt also
to live the life I owe you and find a way to clog-dance,
to jitterbug, to tap or otherwise to jig
on the brilliant ice that is your coffin lid.

27

Imagine all of it, brother, set to such music. The years
of bitterness, your death, the drama of your return
or of your never-having-left – out of sync;
the music, the events, glancing off each other.
The truth is you died with a hole in your shoe
through to your foot, without socks, like poor Dylan
found between the last turning of West Eleventh
and the White Horse Tavern, you on your own bed:
his shoes were worn through the contours to a hole
and a few grains of Laugharne sand, yours
to no grains at all, no love of place nor of anything.
What you shared was a lonely end with similar stuff
boiling in your antibodies – the both of you lost
in the city of self which towered, awaiting the first frost.

28

What you took with you, you must understand,
was a little of your younger brother, and left in him
the much of you which survived the crematorium smoke:
you took from him the counterbalance,
the eleven digits he could have pressed
to hear your voice, but rarely did, left instead
the digits of the wholly unthinkable number.
You left him a life to be led, to be lived for two,
and took with you the rolled up years you'd yet to live:
you left him a hole that went through all floors,
and a fear of certain photographs – you took with you
his loose change, his overcoat, and left him
a weighty discoloured body to shift, much junk to clear
and the panic of not finding you anywhere.

29

You wanted to be feared in life for the silo
of your own body, you wanted to have been born
of worse blood and have straining from one fist
your grim succession of powerful dogs:
something of the wolf in them, the mouth from which
the tongue gagged like a piston on the move
and the breadth of chest and muscle-yoke
drew you down into them, or dragged you along
until it was in question who led the way.
You threw them commands that were thrown through you
but I can recall how once an albedo mist
cast a strange sort of light across your smile
and filled your whole mouth, which was lowered
as if it had never once spoken a word.

30

Bellicose thunder – overhead – rebounds,
eats its own echo, doubles back and talks rudely over us
above the gables of the old hotel. It's pushy
with its interruptions, now soft, now drowning out
all attempts to be heard. The thunder argues
that the clouds, could we see them, bear an unbearable load:
and the deepest bass note of thunder grumbles
through octave after octave until it passes
out of human hearing, and things in the hotel start
to vibrate – the sashes, the filament in the bulb.
Everyone, in every room, looks up anxious
now the thunder is all but indoors. The garden trough
is full of air, the web which traverses it shakes
and first will painfully bend, then break.

31

Now the plucky dead outnumber us at last
the lock-gate of the world lurches up as if the weight at one end
can no longer keep it balanced. All around me the din
of the thunder like boulders being tipped
in the pressure trap of the Mendips – you
are all around me. You might be a single *ohm*
in that rip of lightning or a particle of the black
through which it rips, sound waves that travel.
You might be the hundred-hundredth of a decibel
sounding from firmamental speaker to speaker
and filling the whole hotel, or perhaps every decibel
that cracks open and throws seeds, alive and full
of worldly sounds, of worldly jeopardy – and if
there is government anywhere, you know what it is.

32

You know the turnings beyond the world
that have never been mapped, the pathos of the last street lamp
getting smaller and smaller. You know the truth
of how light divides, how the world slips through
the finest division of light, and is gone.
You know the terror of the peacock which
legs it across the lawn, as the first drops of a million gallons
bounce a leaf, then another – this is how it begins.
The snarl is gone. The flood in the lane will gather
to overwhelm its defences and pick up silt
and the night release new mineral smells
which are cleaner and newer, fresher and more green:
water is air, earth water. Air is fire, and the fire
of water's getting hungry for its reservoir.